Lectionary Hymns For Cycle B

New Hymns For The Church Year Calendar With Old Familiar Tunes

Clyde W. Wentzell

CSS Publishing Company, Inc., Lima, Ohio

LECTIONARY HYMNS FOR CYCLE B

Library of Congress Cataloging-in-Publication Data

Wentzell, Clyde W.
Lectionary hymns for cycle B : new hymns for the church year calendar with old familiar tunes / Clyde W. Wentzell.
p. cm.
ISBN 0-7880-2550-3 (perfect bound : alk. paper)
1. Lutheran Church—Hymns—Texts. 2. Common lectionary (1992). 3. Hymns, English—Texts. I. Title

BV410.W46 2008
264'.23—dc22

2008010687

For more information about CSS Publishing Company resources, visit our website at www.csspub.com or email us at csr@csspub.com or call (800) 241-4056.

Cover design by Barbara Spencer
ISBN-13: 978-0-7880-2550-1
ISBN-10: 0-7880-2550-3

PRINTED IN USA

Dedicated to
St. Matthew's Evangelical Lutheran Church,
Newburne, Nova Scotia,
where I began my faith journey
with my mother at the organ
playing the grand old hymns
of the Christian faith.

Editor's Note

CSS Publishing Company has chosen the option of retaining our Canadian author's spellings of such words as favour, endeavour, Saviour, splendour, and savour, rather than removing the "u" as would be found in the US spellings. We also left metre and centre as is.

Table Of Contents

Introduction

This manuscript contains new words of hymns, metered for singing to familiar hymn tunes.

The Old Testament psalms, plus the gospels, provide church year themes and are the texts of the Revised Common Lectionary, Cycle B, or Year Two, of the three-year cycle of texts used largely by liturgical denominations of churches. Those texts are the source of inspiration for the verses presented here.

Note: Beginning after The Holy Trinity, the psalms in this manuscript are the semi-continuous texts, accepted for use in the Evangelical Lutheran Church in Canada and many mainstream churches in the US.

The hymn tunes recommended may be found in the following: *Lutheran Book of Worship* (LBW), published by Augsburg Publishing House, Minneapolis, Minnesota, copyright 1978; *Service Book and Hymnal* (SBH), of the Lutheran Church in America (Philadelphia), copyright 1958 and endorsed by eight Lutheran church bodies of that time; and *With One Voice* (WOV), a Lutheran resource for worship, published by Augsburg Fortress, Minneapolis, Minnesota, copyright 1995.

O God Up Above

1. O God up above, enthroned with great grace,
Shine forth in your love, revealing your face.
Come to us, O Saviour, give ear to each prayer
And show us your favour, remove our despair.

2. Restore us, O God, and we shall be saved
And publish abroad good news ever craved;
The news of salvation in Jesus the King.
With true adoration, your praises we sing.

3. O Shepherd of all, enthroned up on high,
Give ear as we call, hear your people cry.
How long will you tarry? How long must we wait?
While enemies carry their burdens of hate.

4. Stir up your full might. Oh, come now to save.
Bring us from dark night; make hearts to be brave.
Your light on our pathways shall keep our faith strong
To follow you always, while others may scorn.

5. O Christ on the throne, O King of great might,
We serve you, alone, fighting the good fight.
Assured of your blessing each step of the way,
Your name, thus confessing with grateful hearts pray.

6. Restore us, O Lord, great giver of grace.
God, ever adored, let us see your face.
Shine forth in your glory, a heavenly blaze.
Lord of sacred story, to you be all praise.

Advent 1
Based on Psalm 80:1-7, 16-18
May be sung to HANOVER, 10 10.11 11
LBW 548 — "Oh, Worship The King"

Salvation From Our God

1. Salvation from our God:
The gift of gifts, receive.
The promise made is now fulfilled
In all those who believe.

2. Faithfulness from the ground
Springs up in God's new day,
And righteousness looks from the sky
To join us on the way.

3. We journey in the light
Of God's eternal love,
And those who worship, as is right,
Find peace with God above.

4. God dwells within each heart,
Speaking the message clear,
Of peace, goodwill, where'er God reigns,
Of comfort and good cheer.

5. All praise be to our God,
Who sets the people free.
All fear removed, revived we live,
And thus, God's glory we see.

6. God's path before us lies,
Opened by sins forgiven,
As by the Spirit, ever blest,
Our souls rise up to heaven.

Advent 2
Based on Psalm 85:1-2, 8-13
May be sung to DONCASTER, SM 66.86
SBH 3 — "The Advent Of Our God"

Joyful Hearts Bring Praise

1. Joyful hearts bring praise before you,
Giver of the highest good.
For your bounty we adore you,
Blessed by your rich parenthood.
Laughter sounds from each church steeple;
Joy results from all you do.
God of glory, we, your people,
Live with heartfelt thanks to you.

2. Seeds oft sown by us in sadness,
By your grace, yield peace and joy.
All our weeping turns to gladness
As you, ways of love employ.
Water in the desert flowing,
Brings to life new things of earth;
And all hearts are set aglowing,
In the joy of each new birth.

3. Lord of life, in name, most holy,
Great, the things that you have done.
All our praise is of you, solely,
For you bless us, everyone.
Lord, we come, in each endeavour,
With full joy of heart and voice.
May we give our praise forever
And, in you, always rejoice.

Advent 3 (Joyful Sunday)
Based on Psalm 126
May be sung to HYMN TO JOY, 87.87 D
LBW 551 — "Joyful, Joyful We Adore Thee"

God Of All Generations

1. God of all generations,
   Your covenant holds true.
   O Lord of all the nations,
   We live in praise of you.
   With steadfast love you bless us;
   Forever, shall it be.
   In faithfulness you keep us,
   Throughout eternity.

2. God of all generations,
   From David's ancient line,
   Your Chosen One, most blessed,
   Fulfilled your grand design.
   A throne of grace before us,
   Now marks his reign of love.
   We follow, as descendants,
   All blessed by God above.

3. God of all generations,
   Your word gives strength today.
   As those now gone before us,
   We, too, thrive in your way.
   Your faithfulness in all things,
   From age to age the same,
   Throughout all generations,
   Gives honour to your name.

Advent 4
Based on Psalm 89:1-4, 19-26
May be sung to LANCASHIRE, 76.76 D
LBW 495 — "Lead On, O King Eternal"

Break Forth In Song

1. Break forth in song, let all be glad
   And hail the newborn king!
   Let all the world rejoice and sing.
   Oh, nevermore be sad. Oh, nevermore be sad.
   Oh, never, nevermore be sad.

2. Praise to the Lord who reigns in love,
   In truth and majesty.
   Oh, let the world be led to see
   Our God, who reigns in love, our God who reigns in love,
   Our God, our God who reigns in love.

3. Hail to the king and judge of earth,
   Whose rule is just and right,
   From heaven's throne, coming in might.
   We hail the glad new birth. We hail the glad new birth.
   We hail, we hail the glad new birth.

4. People, rejoice in happy lays.
   Give honour as is due.
   Salvation is God's gift to you.
   Oh, evermore give praise. Oh, evermore give praise.
   Oh, ever, evermore give praise.

Christmas Eve
Based on Psalm 96
May be sung to ANTIOCH, CM with repeat
LBW 39 — "Joy To The World"

Praise To Our God

1. Praise to our God, the one giving us this day to treasure.
   Jesus is with us and heaven is ours in full measure!
   Join in the throng, blending all voices in song,
   Singing God's praises forever.

2. Enthroned on high, hail the Sovereign who rules o'er creation,
   Coming to earth, as a child, bringing to us salvation!
   Heavens proclaim justice and truth in God's name,
   While earth erupts with elation.

3. Coastlands, be glad, while the mountains melt in the Lord's
   presence.
   Fire consumes, darkness fades in the light filled with reverence.
   People, behold! See all God's glory unfold!
   Worshiping God is life's essence.

4. Zion's walls shake, towns of Judah rejoice Christmas morning.
   Jesus is born! All the world thrills on his day now dawning.
   Raised above all, while idols crumble and fall;
   Loving ways, Christ's crown adorning!

Christmas Dawn
Based on Psalm 97
May be sung to LOBE DEN HERREN, 14 14.478
LBW 543 — "Praise To The Lord, The Almighty"

A New Day Is Dawning

1. A new day is dawning, now ended all longing.
   A new song of victory, God's people sing.
   The earth shares the story of God in great glory.
   Today, we behold it in Jesus, the King.
   God's presence to bless us, in love to caress us,
   Unites us as one in the song that we share.
   And all things now living, in praise and thanksgiving,
   Rejoice with assurance we're held in good care.

2. Let all people ponder, in awe, at the wonder
   Of God breaking in, crushing earth's ruthless way.
   God judges with justice, with ways that are righteous:
   A rule that is steadfast, our hope and our stay.
   Oh, may each endeavour, both now and forever,
   Be filled with the joy of the songs that we sing;
   And may God's good favour be ours to savour,
   As onward we go, led by Jesus, the King!

Christmas Day
Based on Psalm 98
May be sung to THE ASH GROVE, 6 6 11.6 6 11 D
LBW 221 — "Sent Forth By God's Blessing"

Jesus Is Born!

1. Jesus is born! Our blessed Saviour!
Joyful, the praise that we bring.
Heaven and earth join in the chorus.
Joyful, the praise that we bring.

Refrain
Let all the universe join in the praise,
Giving all glory to our new king.

2. Angels on high, in mighty anthem,
Share in the praise that we sing.
And from the earth, all creatures praising,
Share in the praise that we sing. *Refrain*

3. Rulers of earth, fall down in worship!
Mighty, the praise that we share.
Both bring young and old, singing together;
Mighty, the praise that we share. *Refrain*

4. Praise, sun and moon, stars in their courses;
Creation's praise without end!
Glory to God, ruling in splendour.
Creation's praise without end. *Refrain*

5. Jesus is King! We are his servants!
Joyful the praise that we sing.
Heaven's best gift, living among us!
Joyful, the praise that we sing. *Refrain*

Christmas 1
Based on Psalm 148
May be sung to EARTH AND ALL STARS, 457.457 with *refrain*
LBW 558 — "Earth And All Stars!"

Come, Let Us Praise The Lord

1. Come, let us praise the Lord,
In songs, with one accord,
Exulting in God's word.
Jerusalem, our home,
And Zion's peaceful dome,
Give praise for God's strong word.

2. In God's word is our strength.
All comes from God at length.
We're blessed through God's own word.
In peace, we're held secure;
Our daily bread made sure;
We're blessed by God's good word.

3. God speaks, and so it's done.
Good news for everyone,
Comes with God's holy word.
All nature stirs around,
Responsive to the sound,
Released through God's own word.

4. Unique, the word God brings,
Whereof, my soul now sings:
God's song, Incarnate Word!
Oh, blessed gift to all,
Comes with the wondrous call
Of God's eternal word.

Christmas 2
Based on Psalm 147:13-21
May be sung to LAUDES DOMINI, 666.666
LBW 546 — "When Morning Gilds The Skies"

God's Light Shines Brightly

1. God's light shines brightly now
For all the world to see.
Oh, come, behold the Christ of God.
Oh, come, behold the Christ of God.
He's king for you and me.
He's king for you and me.

Refrain
Oh, come, see the Baby,
Beautiful, beautiful Baby.
Oh, come, see Jesus the true light,
God's glory and wonder revealed.

2. From near and far they come,
God's people of the earth,
To worship Christ, the newborn king,
To worship Christ, the newborn king,
And hail the wondrous birth.
And hail the wondrous birth. *Refrain*

3. The just and righteous One
We know as God's own Son.
Oh, in his presence let all bow,
Oh, in his presence let all bow,
His reign of peace begun.
His reign of peace begun. *Refrain*

4. The helpless and the poor,
   And those in greatest need,
   Shall know the joy of life restored,
   Shall know the joy of life restored.
   And from all wrong be freed.
   And from all wrong be freed. *Refrain*

The Epiphany Of Our Lord
Based on Psalm 72:1-7, 10-14
May be sung to MARCHING TO ZION, 66.88 with *refrain*
WOV 742 — "Come, We That Love The Lord"

Hear God's Voice In Glory

1. Hear God's voice in glory now,
As before the Lord we bow.
Great, the splendour which God brings,
Shed abroad on dove-like wings,
With mighty voice.

Refrain
Glory, glory, glory, around the throne.
See on earth the reign begun,
Of God's Chosen, blessed Son,
Bestowing peace.

2. Hear the voice of God ring clear:
"My beloved Son" is here.
"Listen to him," blessed to reign,
With great love for all the same,
Wherefore, rejoice. *Refrain*

3. Oh, the wonder that we hear,
As the Lord, our God, draws near.
Over waters dread alarm,
Sounds the Spirit's voice of calm,
That knows no end. *Refrain*

4. Voice of God, enfold us all
With your everlasting call.
May our praises never cease
As we live, blessed by your peace,
Oh, gracious friend. *Refrain*

The Baptism Of Our Lord/Epiphany 1/Ordinary Time 1
Based on Psalm 29
May be sung to CHAUTAUQUA, 77.774 with *refrain*
SBH 234 — "Day Is Dying In The West"

O How Awesome Is God's Wisdom

1. O how awesome is God's wisdom,
How majestic the Lord's ways.
All my thoughts, God holds in secret,
Long before my words of praise.
Lord, you know each path I travel,
Long before the way I've trod;
And my thoughts reach up to heaven,
As I contemplate you, God.

2. Lord, in wonder you have formed me;
Shaped me in my mother's womb;
Brought my inner parts together,
Crafted on your sacred loom.
All your deeds speak of your glory:
Works of intricate design,
Bringing forth in each new creature,
Evidence of the divine.

3. O my gracious God and Saviour,
Blest Creator, hear my prayer,
As I praise you with thanksgiving,
For your tender love and care.
Highest honour, thus bestowing
On you, dearest, truest friend,
As I live with faith's assurance,
You will love me to the end.

Epiphany 2/Ordinary Time 2
Based on Psalm 139:1-5, 12-17
May be sung to ARMSTRONG, 87.87 D
SBH 493 — (second tune) "There's A Wideness In God's Mercy"

In God Alone, Our Hope Is Sure

1. In God alone, our hope is sure,
He is our mighty rock.
In him, each life is held secure.
We're safe within God's flock.

2. In silence, put your trust in him,
Your refuge from all harm.
Let not the light of faith grow dim,
Nor give way to alarm.

3. Deliverance from all that's wrong,
Shall surely come to me.
I'll trust in God my whole life long,
And his salvation see.

4. God is our refuge and our strength,
The keeper of each soul.
Both high and low are his at length,
And under his control.

5. God's steadfast love shall never cease:
His warm embrace, our goal.
He gives the quiet, inner peace,
That makes the spirit whole.

6. O God of love, be with each heart,
Held fast, in prayer, to you.
O God, by strength which you impart,
May we find service true.

Epiphany 3/Ordinary Time 3
Based on Psalm 62:6-14
May be sung to NEW BRITAIN, CM 86.86
(southern harmony)
LBW 448 — "Amazing Grace"

All Praise Be To Our God

1. All praise be to our God,
   Bestowing deeds of grace.
   Coming, firm stem of Jesse's rod,
   Daily, with warm embrace.

2. Ever a source of joy,
   From heaven's lofty throne,
   Great deeds are ever his employ,
   Heaped on his very own.

3. Incarnate God, we view,
   Jesus, High Priest and King;
   Keeping the promise ever true,
   Love gifts unto us bring.

4. Majestic are God's ways;
   Noble, the deeds well done.
   Our highest joy, to give him praise:
   Praise shared by everyone.

5. Quench not the Spirit's fire.
   Resolve, in all you do,
   Sustained by faith, the heart's desire,
   Trust God will be with you.

6. United in one Lord,
   Victorious he lives,
   Wisdom begins with fear of God;
   Xyster-like healing gives.

7. Yield heart and mind and soul,
Zealous for God's ways be.
God's grace can make the spirit whole,
With peace and liberty.

Epiphany 4/Ordinary Time 4
Based on Psalm 111
May be sung to FRANCONIA, SM 66.86
LBW 22 — "The Advent Of Our God"

Note: This hymn is presented as an acrostic, conveying the concept from the Hebrew, where the psalm takes on an alphabetic acrostic pattern in which every other verse begins with a successive letter of the alphabet.

Sing Praise To God

1. Sing praise to God, tell of God's wondrous glory;
   Tell of his deeds revered in sacred story.
   Tell how his loving leads to deeds of caring,
   Grace ever sharing.

2. Great is the Lord, and full of understanding;
   In every act of kindness, love commanding.
   The troubled are raised up, the wicked grounded,
   And praise is sounded.

3. The stars are named and fixed within their courses.
   All nature stirs, responsive to God's forces.
   Earth's creatures find their food, a gift from heaven,
   And wrongs forgiven.

4. The steadfast love of God endures forever.
   To live in awe of God earns his good pleasure.
   Praise to the Lord we give for heaven's treasure:
   Ours in full measure.

5. Praise God and give him thanks for every blessing.
   All hope is fixed in God, our needs addressing.
   We sing praise to the Lord, our chief endeavour,
   Now and forever.

Epiphany 5/Ordinary Time 5
Based on Psalm 147:1-12, 21
May be sung to WOJTKIEWIECZ, 11 11 11.5
LBW 393 — "Rise, Shine, You People!"

O Lord, Hear My Praying

Refrain
O Lord, hear my praying;
O Lord, hear my praying;
O my Lord, hear my praying,
Burdened in my soul I call.

1. Give praise unto the Lord,
   For he restores to life his own.
   Yes, he heals the broken heart,
   Grants salvation to us all. *Refrain*

2. Give praise, as ever due,
   For he restores to life his own,
   Yes, he heals the broken heart,
   Grants salvation to us all. *Refrain*

3. Give praise forevermore
   For he restores to life his own.
   Yes, he heals the broken heart,
   Grants salvation to us all. *Refrain*

4. O Lord, I trust in you,
   For you're my helper in all need.
   Yes, you grant each soul's request,
   And in righteous paths you lead. *Refrain*

Epiphany 6/Ordinary Time 6
Based on Psalm 30
May be sung to BURLEIGH, 68.77 with *refrain*
WOV 627 — "My Lord, What A Morning"

God Of Mercy, Ever Blessing

1. God of mercy, ever blessing,
Tending to each human need,
Lo, we come, our sins confessing:
Wrongs we've done by thought and deed.
Ever blessing! Ever blessing!
God of love. This is our creed.

2. God, you show to us great favour;
Your protecting care we know.
Life restored is ours to savour,
As you, saving grace bestow.
Everlasting! Everlasting
In your pathway let us go.

3. God, when enemies would hound us;
When their ways trouble us sore;
Gracious God, O then surround us,
With your love, the more and more.
Ever blessing! Ever blessing!
Is the God whom we adore.

4. Bless us, Lord, both now and ever,
Dwelling with us all our days.
Oh, may we forsake you, never,
But a thankful chorus raise.
Everlasting! Everlasting!
From our hearts we give you praise.

Epiphany 7/Ordinary Time 7
Based on Psalm 41
May be sung to PRAISE MY SOUL, 87.87.87
LBW 549 — "Praise, My Soul, The King Of Heaven"

Bless The Lord With Songs Unceasing

1. Bless the Lord with songs unceasing,
   Bless God for great love and care.
   O my soul, with praise increasing,
   Celebrate with joyous flair.
   In the praise of God, together,
   All as one, a chorus raise,
   To our God, in fullest measure,
   Who deserves our highest praise.

2. Thank you, God, for every blessing,
   Ruling o'er the church in love;
   In your gracious arms, caressing
   Those who seek your courts above.
   In forgiveness, and with healing,
   All your works of mercy crown;
   Wondrous ways, ever revealing:
   Great Redeemer of renown.

3. Bless the Lord, full of compassion,
   Satisfying all with good;
   Giving help of every fashion,
   In the way of parenthood.
   All creation, in thanksgiving,
   Shares in praising God above.
   As he gives us strength for living,
   We extol his steadfast love.

Epiphany 8/Ordinary Time 8
Based on Psalm 103:1-13, 22
May be sung to NETTLETON, 87.87 D
LBW 499 — "Come, Thou Fount Of Every Blessing"

What A Sight To See, On The Mountaintop

1. What a sight to see, on the mountaintop,
   There, the mighty God, our Lord, behold.
   What a voice to hear, causing hearts to stop,
   As God summons earth with visions bold.

   Refrain
   Glory, glory, out of Zion
   Beams wondrous light.
   Glory, glory, Transfiguration shows
   All is right.

2. Our God comes to us, awesome, in great might,
   Calling far and wide for all to hear,
   As the faithful ones, judged by God aright,
   In his presence know there's naught to fear. *Refrain*

3. What peace comes our way, as on God we wait,
   Earth and heaven in God's glory shine,
   And the word of God, never shall abate,
   Spreading faith and truth, in joy divine. *Refrain*

The Transfiguration Of Our Lord
(Last Sunday After Epiphany)
Based on Psalm 50:1-6
May be sung to SHOWALTER, 10 9.10 9 with *refrain* 48, 49
WOV 780 — "What A Fellowship, What A Joy Divine"

Have Mercy, Lord, I Cry

1. Have mercy, Lord, I cry,
   Lord, hear my every sigh,
   Forgive my sin.
   Wash all my guilt away;
   Mercy and love convey,
   As I walk your way,
   Give peace within.

2. Create new life in me,
   From evil set me free;
   Renew my soul.
   Restore my joy again;
   By grace, my faith sustain.
   Let me not hope in vain,
   But make me whole.

3. In gladness let me hear
   Assurance you are near;
   Lord, set me right.
   Speak to me words of love,
   Spirit, most holy dove;
   Send pardon from above.
   Give me new sight.

4. For all your gracious ways,
O Lord, receive my praise
With humble heart.
Contrite, the prayers I make,
Ever for your name's sake.
Bless, Lord, the way I take,
Doing my part.

Ash Wednesday
Based on Psalm 51:1-18
May be sung to OLIVET, 664.6664
SBH 375 — "My Faith Looks Up To Thee"

To You, O Lord, Most Holy

(O God Of My Salvation)

1. To you, O Lord, most holy,
   I turn in every need.
   I trust in you to guide me,
   And shape my every deed.
   O God of my salvation,
   Providing constant love,
   Come, teach me, Lord, and lead me,
   Blest Spirit, holy dove.

2. Oh, may I ever follow
   The pathways you make known.
   Your truth be my companion,
   Your words become my own.
   O God of my salvation,
   Forgive my wanton sin.
   Blot out all my transgressions
   And make me pure within.

3. O good and upright Saviour,
   In prayer I wait on you.
   Your faithfulness I treasure;
   Your words I know are true.
   O God of my salvation,
   Uphold me in your ways,
   That I may live and ever,
   Ever show forth your praise.

Lent 1

Based on Psalm 25:1-9

May be sung to BRED DI NA VIAA VINGAR, 76.76 D

WOV 741 — "Thy Holy Wings" (Swedish folk tune)

People Of God, In Holy Fear

1. People of God, in holy fear,
   Give forth great praise in worship here.
   Stand firm in faith with hearts of love,
   Giving all praise to God above.

2. God hears each sigh, and answers prayer.
   Jesus is pleased, our lot to share.
   In God, the Lord, all praise is due.
   Lord of the church, our thanks to you.

3. Joyous thanksgiving be to God;
   Saviour and King, ever adored.
   Let us, as one, in joy exult,
   For all the blessings God has wrought.

4. Give God all glory to his name;
   From age to age, ever the same.
   By God shall all the world be blest,
   And find in him, eternal rest.

5. With heart and voice, our praise we bring;
   Loud alleluias, too, we sing.
   Glory to God, our song shall be,
   Now, and throughout eternity.

Lent 2
Based on Psalm 22:22-30
May be sung to DUKE STREET, LM
LBW 530 — "Jesus Shall Reign"

Creation Bears The Sight Of God's Eternal Light

(A Glory Without End)

1. Creation bears the sight
   Of God's eternal light:
   A glory without end.
   God's work is on display,
   Proclaimed by night and day:
   God's glory knows no end.

2. The heavens, truth proclaim,
   All glory to God's name:
   A glory without end.
   Across heaven's vast dome,
   The sun displays its home:
   God's glory knows no end.

3. No speech conveys the thought
   Of all that God has wrought:
   A glory without end.
   Yet, God's great work is done;
   The wonder is passed on:
   God's glory knows no end.

4. God's law is perfect light,
   Revealing what is right:
   A glory without end.
   Commandments sound the praise
   Of God's eternal ways:
   God's glory knows no end.

5. The laws of God convey
Truth worthy to obey:
A glory without end.
Great riches they display,
Forever and for aye:
God's glory without end.

6. My God, I make my prayer:
Your glory may I share?
A glory without end.
Redeemer, ever true,
May all things that you do:
Give glory without end.

Lent 3
Based on Psalm 19
May be sung to LAUDES DOMINI, 666.666
SBH 416 — "When Morning Gilds The Skies"

O Give Thanks Unto The Lord

1. O give thanks unto the Lord
   for all the wonders he has done.
   Praise the Lord for every blessing,
   let us praise him, everyone;
   For he heard the people's crying,
   and his healing was begun:
   Praise God for steadfast love.

   Refrain
   Praise the Lord, give thanks and glory!
   Praise the Lord, give thanks and glory!
   Praise the Lord, give thanks and glory!
   Praise God for steadfast love.

2. When the people neared the gates of death,
   weighed down in sinful ways;
   In distress they cried unto the Lord,
   as one, a prayer to raise.
   Then God's word went out, and healing them
   gave cause for joyous praise:
   Praise God for steadfast love. *Refrain*

3. With the Lord we know forgiveness
   and redemption in his name,
   All his works are known both far and wide;
   his goodness we proclaim.
   As we live with that assurance,
   he remains ever the same.
   Praise God for steadfast love. *Refrain*

Lent 4
Based on Psalm 107:1-3, 17-22
May be sung to BATTLE HYMN, 15 15 15.6 with *refrain*
LBW 332 — "Battle Hymn Of The Republic"

My Life Is Fashioned By God's Word

1. My life is fashioned by God's word,
So full of grace and wonder,
As with my whole heart, truth I seek;
Your teaching, Lord, I ponder.

Refrain
Your word, O God, holds me secure;
It is my soul's chief treasure.
Christ in my life, my utmost need,
Given in fullest measure.

2. In meditation, oft I'm found,
Seeking your way to follow;
Delighting in your law, I'm bound
To bypass all that's hollow. *Refrain*

3. Lord, free me from all senseless thought;
Save me from ways of sinning;
Give me a heart to praise you, Lord,
And set my life to winning. *Refrain*

4. O Christ, my Lord, pray with me go.
May I forsake you, never.
From youth to ages yet unborn,
My lips will praise you, ever. *Refrain*

Lent 5
Based on Psalm 119:9-16
May be sung to HOW CAN I KEEP FROM SINGING, 87.87 with *refrain*
WOV 781 — "My Life Flows On In Endless Song"

Unto The Lord Be Praise

(Waving Palm Branches)

1. Unto the Lord be praise and blessing as is due.
Let all a joyous chorus raise.
Let all a joyous chorus raise.
Christ reigns in love for you.
Christ reigns in love for you.

Refrain
We're waving palm branches,
Welcoming, welcoming Jesus.
Hosannas of praise to Jesus,
Our beautiful Saviour and King.

2. The gates swing open wide, the righteous enter in.
Oh, give God praise on every side.
Oh, give God praise on every side.
He saves us from all sin.
He saves us from all sin. *Refrain*

3. This is the day of days, shedding abroad God's light.
As we behold his sun-like rays,
As we behold his sun-like rays,
His paths all gleaming bright.
His paths all gleaming bright. *Refrain*

4. Blessed the One who comes in God's most holy name.
To you, O Lord, we shout in joy.
To you, O Lord, we shout in joy.
And rally to your call.
And rally to your call. *Refrain*

5. So give thanks to the Lord, recall his steadfast love.
   Extol Christ's name with one accord.
   Extol Christ's name with one accord.
   Our mighty cornerstone.
   Our mighty cornerstone. *Refrain*

Palm Sunday
Based on Psalm 118:1-2, 19-29
May be sung to MARCHING TO ZION, 66.86 with *refrain*
WOV 742 — "Come, We That Love The Lord"

Alas! I'm Sunken In Despair

1. Alas! I'm sunken in despair,
   Twice burdened with my grief;
   A life distraught beyond repair;
   A soul beyond relief.

2. Oh, see my days in sorrow spent,
   Forsaken and cast down;
   While enemies will not relent,
   Scorn is my bitter crown.

3. A broken vessel, useless pot,
   Forgotten and alone;
   I seek, in vain, a resting spot,
   A solace all my own.

4. Just so, my Lord, his passion bore,
   For sin he did atone;
   Rejection, cruel grief most sore,
   In love, suffered alone.

5. Christ's love makes faith spring into life,
   And sees all fears depart,
   As trusting God amid all strife,
   Strength burns within my heart.

6. O Lord, upon your servant shine,
   Favour and grace renew,
   With steadfast love: the glory thine.
   All praise and thanks to you.

Sunday Of The Passion
Based on Psalm 31:9-16
May be sung to MARTYRDOM, CM 86.86
LBW 98 — "Alas! And Did My Saviour Bleed"

O Lord, My God

Refrain
O Lord, my God,
Pray, what shall I do
To show thanks to you
For bounty I have from you?

1. This is what I vow to do:
Lift up my prayer unto you;
Pour out libations of trust, that's true. *Refrain*

2. Calling upon your great name,
Proclaim the truth of your fame:
Faithfully serving us all the same. *Refrain*

3. Blessed by the freedom you give,
Loosed from all bonds, thus to live;
Thanksgiving sacrifice, rich votive. *Refrain*

4. Serving you, Lord, serving all,
Obedient to your call,
Knowing your presence and love, stand tall. *Refrain*

Maundy Thursday
Based on Psalm 116:1, 10-17
May be sung to CHEREPONI, (irregular with *refrain*) (Ghanaian folk tune)
WOV 765 — "Jesu, Jesu, Fill Us With Your Love"

The Darkness Sweeps Around Me

1. The darkness sweeps around me;
   Anguish on me descends;
   Despair and grief confound me;
   I search in vain for friends.
   Your silence, God, I ponder;
   Your absence in my need.
   Forsaken, left to wonder,
   Why God, do you not heed?

2. In my distress and anguish,
   By night and day I cry.
   Why am I left to languish?
   Why do you not reply?
   How different, in our hist'ry,
   Deliverance you gave.
   Now, shrouded with deep myst'ry
   Why, God, do you not save?

3. The scorn that marked Christ's passion;
   The life that he laid down,
   'Twas all for my transgression:
   Both cross and thorn-filled crown.
   Oh, what a faithless story
   My human frame portrays.
   To Christ be all the glory;
   To Christ be all the praise.

4. The leap of faith has brought me,
Through all life's bitter pain,
To trust the Christ who sought me,
In death, to live again.
O Christ, through your behaviour
Of sacrificial love,
I've come to know my Saviour,
And bless my God above.

Good Friday

Based on Psalm 22

May be sung to PASSION CHORALE, 76.76 D

SBH 88 — (second tune) "O Sacred Head, Now Wounded"

God, All Praise We Give To The Saviour

Refrain
God, all praise we give to the Saviour,
Dying and rising, giving us new life.
Son of God, pointing toward heaven,
All praise to you, steadfast in love.

1. Lord, you are good, all your works show your glory;
You are the sun shining forth in the night.
True to your word, you have made us new people.
All praise to you, steadfast in love. *Refrain*

2. Lord, you are good, ever doing great wonders.
By your strong word, you created all things.
Heavens abound, light of light to us beaming.
All praise to you, steadfast in love. *Refrain*

3. Lord, you are good, you remembered our weakness.
Christ of the cross, in our midst, lead the way.
Servant of all, you redeemed us and keep us.
All praise to you, steadfast in love. *Refrain*

4. Lord, you are good, and to you be all honour:
Heaven's great God, thanks and praise be to you!
Love is the word that defines you forever.
All praise to you, steadfast in love. *Refrain*

Vigil Of Easter
Based on Psalm 136:1-9, 23-26
May be sung to BERNADETTE FARRELL, 11 10.11 8 with *refrain*
WOV 614 — "Praise To You, O Christ, Our Saviour"

All Praise, This Easter Day!

1. All praise, this Easter Day!
Good news: The Saviour lives!
Oh, worship Christ with heart and voice,
For the new life he gives.

Refrain
Rejoice! Be glad!
Give thanks! Our Saviour lives!

2. This is the festive day,
Banishing all our fears.
Glad songs of victory we sing
As Christ's new day appears. *Refrain*

3. Because our Saviour lives,
This new life we have, too;
Christ died, but rose to live on high,
To share his life anew. *Refrain*

4. The gates are open wide!
The righteous enter in,
Free from all guilt and senseless pride,
Freed by Christ's death for sin. *Refrain*

5. The stone rejected long,
Is the chief cornerstone.
All stones of death are rolled away;
We worship Christ alone. *Refrain*

6. "I shall not die, but live;
The deeds of God recall."
I'll spread the gospel while I live,
Of Christ's love for us all. *Refrain*

7. O come, dear Christian friends,
Good news let all employ:
This Easter Day the Lord has made,
To fill our hearts with joy! *Refrain*

Easter Day
Based on Psalm 118:1-2, 14-24
May be sung to MARION, SM with *refrain*
LBW 553 — "Rejoice, O Pilgrim Throng!"

God's Wonders Unfold

1. God's wonders unfold as glory we see,
   Shaking the earth's foundation.
   The sea looked and fled, the waters turned back.
   God gave his people salvation.

   Refrain
   To walk with Christ, gives gladness of heart,
   His presence, a light by night, by day.
   Jesus shines upon us, never to depart.
   Living Lord, light up my way.

2. The Lord, in wonder, made the sea to flee;
   The waters reeled, receding.
   Mountains and hills skipped like ewes with their lambs;
   Creation, God's will achieving. *Refrain*

3. Tremble, O earth, at the presence of God;
   The God who gave us Jesus.
   Of all the ways people look to be saved,
   Christians know the way is Jesus. *Refrain*

Easter Evening
Based on Psalm 114
May be sung to HOUSTON, 10 7.10 8 with *refrain*
WOV 649 — "I Want To Walk As A Child Of The Light"

God Calls Us All

1. God calls us all to live in peace,
Knowing the joy that ne'er shall cease.
To live as one, this is God's call,
To rally 'round his sacred hall.

Refrain
In unity and love to be,
Both now and to eternity.

2. Like precious oil poured on the head,
In life renewed, as from the dead.
How good and pleasant is this life
When lived in Christ, free from all strife. *Refrain*

3. With Christ, the Lord, we're lifted up;
Removed, is every bitter cup.
And thus to know the holy thrill,
Of standing on God's sacred hill. *Refrain*

4. Our life together, by God's grace,
Secures for us a resting place.
All the redeemed on God's bright shore;
Shall know sweet joys forevermore. *Refrain*

5. Like dew from Herman's lofty height,
Mount Zion conjures up the sight
Of kindred knowing they're to be
Blessed by the Lord with life that's free. *Refrain*

Easter 2
Based on Psalm 133
May be sung to MELITA, 88.88.88 with *refrain*
LBW 294 — "My Hope Is Built On Nothing Less"

O God, In Deep Distress I Pray

1. O God, in deep distress I pray.
   I seek the solace of your way,
   Longing, in faith, to know sweet rest,
   Assured you grant me what is best.

2. You hear and answer when I call;
   Your gift of peace, spread like a pall.
   You set apart, from all that's wrong,
   The faithful who, to you, belong.

3. Lord, you put gladness in my heart.
   May I ne'er from your truth depart;
   But ever offer you my love,
   And ever trust you, God of love.

4. The needs of many rise in prayer,
   Hoping some goodness they may share,
   And see the light of God's fair face,
   Trusting his mercy; saved by grace.

5. Blessed with the peace, O Lord, you give,
   Now in your service, let me live.
   In day and night time may I be
   Held safe, and from all care be free.

Easter 3
Based on Psalm 4
May be sung to MARYTON, LM 88.88
LBW 492 — "O Master, Let Me Walk With You"

O My Good Shepherd

1. O my Good Shepherd, O Lord of my soul,
   Keep me forever beneath your control.
   In right paths lead me for your name's sake.
   All the best choices, Lord, help me to make.

2. When through dark valleys my walk is severe,
   Keep me from evil, Lord, ever be near.
   Your rod and staff, my discipline be,
   O my Good Shepherd, keep watch over me.

3. You spread a table of bountiful store.
   Rich are your mercies and love evermore.
   Oil on the head, anointing most pure,
   Flows in abundance as your love is sure.

4. In all you give me, O Lord, hear my praise.
   Shepherd most faithful today and always.
   Freely you give; my cup overflows;
   Nothing but blessings your caring bestows.

5. Surely your goodness and mercy will be,
   Now and forever, your dealing with me,
   And I shall be in God's house alway;
   Christ, my Good Shepherd, my confident stay.

Easter 4
Based on Psalm 23
May be sung to SLANE, 10 10.9 10 (Irish tune)
WOV 776 — "Be Thou My Vision"

Praise The Lord, Great God Above

1. Praise the Lord, great God above.
   Praise God for his deeds of love.

   Refrain
   Glorify God everyone,
   Marvel at all God has done.

2. Our salvation is procured;
   For our sake, great pain endured. *Refrain*

3. Those who sleep beneath the earth,
   Shall awake to glad new birth. *Refrain*

4. Praise the Lord for answered prayer.
   See his rule spread everywhere. *Refrain*

5. Live we ever with the Lord:
   Feared and awesome, yet adored. *Refrain*

6. Worship God and serve him, too;
   All good things he does for you. *Refrain*

7. Praise the Lord by whom we live;
   Thanks and adoration give. *Refrain*

Easter 5
Based on Psalm 22:24-30
May be sung to MONKLAND, 77.77 (Moravian melody)
SBH 405 — "Let Us, With A Gladsome Mind"

Sing We, To The Lord Of Glory

1. Sing we, to the Lord of glory;
Sing a joyous, glad new song.
Tell again, the wondrous story:
Praise and thanks to God belong.
For the victory Christ bought us,
Shed abroad in steadfast love;
For the blessings he has brought us,
We give thanks to God above.

2. Marvelous, and full of splendour,
Are the works the Lord has done.
Joyous, now, the praise we render,
For his grace to everyone.
Let the trumpet and the lyre,
And the horn join in the praise.
Spread the story like a fire,
Warming hearts to endless days.

3. Sing the new song, all creation;
Sing the praise of God above.
Earth and sea and every nation,
Join the song of wondrous love.
See our sovereign Lord before us;
Hail the Saviour, loud and long.
All together, in one chorus,
Sing the joyous, glad new song.

Easter 6
Based on Psalm 98
May be sung to HYMN TO JOY, 87.87 D
LBW 551 — "Joyful, Joyful We Adore Thee"

To The Lord Of Lords, Ascended

1. To the Lord of lords, ascended,
   Come we, now, with songs of praise.
   All his works are well attended,
   Truth and justice mark his ways.
   Christ the victor, crowned in glory,
   Now and evermore shall be.
   Now and evermore shall be.

2. Clap your hands, applaud him solely.
   Awesome is the Lord we own.
   None can claim his place most holy,
   He, alone, deserves the throne.
   Christ the victor, crowned in glory,
   Giving peace to every soul.
   Giving peace to every soul.

3. Sing we praise, and shout in gladness,
   To the King of all the earth.
   Christ has cleared away all sadness,
   Giving us joyous rebirth.
   Christ the victor, crowned in glory,
   Reigning in each thankful heart.
   Reigning in each thankful heart.

4. Christ, who rules over all nations,
   Claims us as his heritage;
   From our many, varied stations,
   Makes us one of every age.
   Christ the victor, crowned in glory:
   Laud him now and evermore.
   Laud him now and evermore.

The Ascension Of Our Lord
Based on Psalm 47
May be sung to CWM RHONDDA, 87.87.877
LBW 415 — "God Of Grace And God Of Glory"

Happy Are The Ones Who In The Lord Live

1. Happy are the ones who in the Lord live,
Delighting in his pathway of life;
Who stand firm, trusting in God,
Against all that's evil, causing strife.

Refrain
And you will yield much fruit,
Fed by fresh streams;
Growing tall at God's right hand.
So shall you evermore live,
Refreshed by God's Spirit every day.

2. Delight in the law, delight in God's ways,
While loving all that God commands.
Let right ways ever abound.
Give way to the Spirit's just demands. *Refrain*

3. The Lord watches o'er those doing the right;
Who follow not the path that is wrong.
Eternal, the life they share,
And ever in the Lord shall be strong. *Refrain*

Easter 7
Based on Psalm 1
May be sung to ON EAGLE'S WINGS (irregular)
WOV 779 — "You Who Dwell In The Shelter Of The Lord"

Let Us Watch And Wait With Jesus

1. Let us watch and wait for Jesus,
To fulfill his promise fair,
When the Spirit comes and frees us
From each burden of despair.

Refrain
Yes, we'll watch and wait God's coming,
A beautiful and wondrous sight to see:
Dove-like, the Holy Spirit's coming;
Breath of life for you and me.

2. All our hope is fixed in Jesus;
His the glory and the crown.
On the cross he died to save us;
His, the vict'ry of renown. *Refrain*

3. When the light descends from heaven,
Then behold God's steadfast love,
Filling each soul as a leaven;
Comforter, most holy dove. *Refrain*

4. Soon our waiting will be over;
All our wondering shall cease,
And the Lord's own hand will hover,
With the promised gift of peace. *Refrain*

Pentecost Vigil
Based on Psalm 33:12-22
May be sung to HANSON PLACE, 87.87 with *refrain*
WOV 690 — "Shall We Gather At The River"

Holy Spirit, Sent From Heaven

1. Holy Spirit, sent from heaven,
   Breathing new life all around;
   As yeast placed, a more sure leaven,
   You create a sacred ground.
   Holy Spirit, Holy Spirit,
   In your truth may we be found.
   In your truth may we be found.

2. May your story be forever,
   God of glory, Lord of might.
   May your Word forsake us, never,
   And your Spirit keep all right.
   Sanctify us for your service,
   Breathe in us life-giving fire.
   Breathe in us life-giving fire.

3. I will sing your wondrous story,
   Praising you, O God of love.
   I will meditate in glory
   And rejoice in heaven's dove.
   All the works of God, abounding,
   Join in showing forth God's praise.
   Join in showing forth God's praise.

4. Spread your goodness all around us;
Free us all from sin's control.
Let not evil's ways confound us,
But renew each sin-sick soul.
Thus, equipped for praise-filled living,
We will bless you evermore.
We will bless you evermore.

The Day Of Pentecost
Based on Psalm 104:25-35, 37
May be sung to CWM RHONDDA, 87.87.877
LBW 343 — "Guide Me Ever, Great Redeemer"

God Our Creator

(God Of All Glory)

1. God, our Creator, source of all strength,
   All that we are, comes from your hand at length.
   Yours be the glory, yours be the might,
   Squelching the darkness, giving the light.

   Refrain
   God of all glory, trusted and true,
   This is our story: All praise to you.
   God of all glory, trusted and true,
   This is our story: All praise to you.

2. Blessed Redeemer, saving the lost,
   Giving new life, never counting the cost.
   Words of assurance, you ever give,
   Sealing our faith as daily we live. *Refrain*

3. O Sanctifier, giver of peace;
   making us one in a joy ne'er to cease.
   Flames ever flashing, purge as by fire,
   Fit us for heaven, our soul's desire. *Refrain*

4. Praise we the Father, praise we the Son;
   Praise Holy Spirit; great God, three in one.
   Give we the glory to your blest name;
   Now and forever, always the same. *Refrain*

The Holy Trinity
Based on Psalm 29
May be sung to ASSURANCE, 9 10.99 with *refrain*
WOV 699 — "Blessed Assurance"

O Lord, Before Your Throne Of Grace

1. O Lord, before your throne of grace
   We come in humble prayer.
   How good to contemplate your face,
   As you, our burdens share.

2. In times of trouble, when we pray,
   You answer each request,
   Giving support and help away,
   And all of heaven's best.

3. Grant, gracious Lord, our heart's desire;
   All goodly plans fulfill.
   May worship be a cleansing fire;
   Our gifts cast to your will.

4. In you, O Lord, we find our joy,
   And set banners on high;
   In your name, heart and soul employ,
   To shout our fullest cry.

5. We trust you, Lord, for answered prayer,
   Assured that what you give
   Is your blest presence with each care,
   As by your grace, we live.

6. Your victory shall be our song,
   Whene'er on you we call.
   Oh, keep us, ever, in faith, strong;
   And bless us one and all.

Proper 6/Pentecost 4/Ordinary Time 11
Based on Psalm 20
May be sung to NAOMI, CM
SBH 458 — "Prayer Is The Soul's Sincere Desire"

Rise, Sovereign Lord

Refrain
Rise, sovereign Lord,
Be the stronghold of all your people.
Rule, Jesus, rule.
God, we trust in you.
Show forth your might;
Triumph over the nations' evil.
Reveal yourself, Lord, in all that is right.

1. Lord, your name is revered among us,
   As the truth of your word shines on us.
   Lord of life, you alone are the story;
   All our praises redound to your glory.
   Rise up, Lord. Rise up, Lord. *Refrain*

2. As we sing unto you our praises,
   Hear the song that your church now raises;
   As we rejoice in your great salvation,
   Gracious God, fill our hearts with elation.
   Rise up, Lord. Rise up, Lord. *Refrain*

Proper 7/Pentecost 5/Ordinary Time 12
Based on Psalm 9:9-20
May be sung to SHINE, JESUS, SHINE, 99 10.10 33 with *refrain*
WOV 651 — "Shine, Jesus, Shine"

I Wait For You, O Lord

1. I wait for you, O Lord, I wait,
   My soul awaits in hope.
   Out of the depths I cry to you:
   My needs are vast in scope.
   Oh, hear the prayers of all your saints,
   Who call upon your name.
   Remove from us all pain and care,
   Restore to life again.

2. If you should count the cost of sin,
   What price ought we to pay?
   But, by your Son the debt is paid,
   And hope is here to stay.
   Forgiveness is the gift you share,
   O Lord of love and grace.
   We rest assured, as by your cross,
   We know your warm embrace.

3. O people of the Lord, rejoice,
   Hope always in the Lord,
   For Christ has power to redeem:
   He is the one adored.
   The steadfast love of God, we own;
   His praise shall ever be.
   A new day dawns, bright as the sun,
   Unto eternity.

Proper 8/Pentecost 6/Ordinary Time 13
Based on Psalm 130
May be sung to KINGSFOLD, CMD
WOV 730 — "My Soul Proclaims Your Greatness"

Oh, The Glory Of Our God

1. Oh, the glory of our God,
   Now, and evermore, adored.
   Beautiful, your holy hill,
   Shining forth your gracious will.
   You defend against all wrong,
   In your Spirit, keep us strong.

2. Lord, we ponder your great love:
   Yours, the name, all names above.
   In the church we sing your praise.
   We rejoice throughout our days.
   Yours, the vict'ry held in store;
   Yours, the glory evermore.

3. Look we up, beyond the sky,
   To behold our God on high.
   In the city of our king,
   Of Mount Zion, let us sing.
   Its defenses are secure;
   All its ways, therein, are pure.

4. Tell the good news, let it ring,
   Of our gracious Lord and king.
   Let the generations know,
   God is great, with whom we go.
   This is God, our Lord above,
   Now and ever, God of love.

Proper 9/Pentecost 7/Ordinary Time 14
Based on Psalm 48
May be sung to TOPLADY, 77.77.77
SBH 379 — (second tune) "Rock Of Ages"

Oh, Come Before The Lord

1. Oh, come before the Lord, rejoice,
And give God praise with cheerful voice.
Stand in his presence, one and all,
Fed by his grace, each one, stand tall.

Refrain
Before the King of Glory, stand,
Tell of his fame throughout the land:
God saves us with his mighty hand.

2. Who is the King of great renown?
Who is the one who wears the crown?
The King of Glory, is his name,
From age to age, ever the same. *Refrain*

3. Ascend the hill of God, the Lord,
All things are his; the one adored.
Receive the blessing which God gives:
Eternity, the life he lives. *Refrain*

4. The doors and gates are open wide,
That all may with the Lord abide,
And, standing in God's sacred place,
May gaze upon his holy face. *Refrain*

Proper 10/Pentecost 8/Ordinary Time 15
Based on Psalm 24
May be sung to THE SOLID ROCK, 88.88 88 8 with *refrain*
LBW 293 — "My Hope Is Built On Nothing Less"

Oh, The Love Of God Is Endless

1. Oh, the love of God is endless,
Caring for us every day;
In his loving arms he bears us,
Keeps us lest we go astray.
Oh, what joy to know the Saviour
Who supplies our every need;
As a shepherd, gently leads us,
Love flows from each kindly deed.

2. God, the rock of our salvation,
Loving parent of each child;
In your name we live as family;
There, we find your presence, mild.
Steadfast is your word of promise,
Never changed, forever true.
Faithfulness remains the watchword,
As our trust is fixed in you.

3. All God's ways reflect the promise,
In the covenant of grace.
In his name, the strength is given,
For each burden that we face.
Praise we give for every blessing,
Resting on us like a dove.
All of life is our thanksgiving
To you, gracious God of love.

Proper 11/Pentecost 9/Ordinary Time 16
Based on Psalm 89:20-37
May be sung to ARMSTRONG, 87.87 D
SBH 493 — "There's A Wideness In God's Mercy"

In This World So Full Of Evil

1. In this world so full of evil,
   God, I make my prayer:
   In the midst of life's confusion,
   May I find you there.

   Refrain
   Hear me, Jesus, when I call to you.
   Give your word of reassurance:
   "I will be with you."

2. Fools may make the false assertion,
   That there is no God;
   Straying in perverse delusion
   Knowing not the Lord. *Refrain*

3. Praying in anticipation,
   Help, you will provide;
   Lord, I bow in faith, well-knowing,
   You are by my side. *Refrain*

4. God sends help from out of Zion;
   Fortunes are restored,
   Causing joy and exaltation:
   Heaven's rich reward. *Refrain*

Proper 12/Pentecost 10/Ordinary Time 17
Based on Psalm 14
May be sung to PASS ME NOT, 85.85 with *refrain*
SBH 461 — "Pass Me Not, O Gentle Saviour"

Cleanse Me, O Lord

1. Cleanse me, O Lord, free me from sin,
O make my spirit pure within.
May I, each deed, with you begin.
O Saviour God, cleanse me, cleanse me.

2. Cleanse me, O Lord, your contrite child.
Merciful Jesus, meek and mild,
Make me your servant undefiled.
O Saviour God, cleanse me, cleanse me.

3. Cleanse me, O Lord of steadfast love,
Send down your pardon from above,
Descending, peaceful, as a dove.
O Saviour God, cleanse me, cleanse me.

4. Cleanse me, O Lord, renew my heart,
Grant joy that never will depart,
Refreshed, each day, for a new start.
O Saviour God, cleanse me, cleanse me.

5. Cleanse me, O Lord, that I may live,
Sustained by the every grace you give;
Assured you ever will forgive.
O Saviour God, cleanse me, cleanse me.

6. Cleanse me, O Lord, of sins you know,
That I, in blindness do not show.
Lord, Spirit-led, help me to grow.
O Saviour God, cleanse me, cleanse me.

Proper 13/Pentecost 11/Ordinary Time 18
Based on Psalm 51:1-12
May be sung to WOODWORTH, LM
LBW 296 — "Just As I Am, Without One Plea"

God, Hear My Plea

1. God, hear my plea as unto you I cry.
   From deep despair, Lord, hear my every sigh.
   I call to you, assured you care for me.
   Grant your forgiveness, God, hear my plea.

2. I wait for you, O Lord, for you I wait,
   Trusting your grace to free me from sin's weight.
   No one but you, O Lord, can set me free.
   Breathe new life in my soul, God, hear my plea.

3. Your word gives hope, and courage to go on.
   A night of prayer gives way to morning's sun.
   Renewed in faith, my song shall ever be:
   Hold me within your palm, God, hear my plea.

4. Redemption shall God, to his people give;
   Freed from iniquities, in him we live.
   Knowing God's favour, fills the heart with glee.
   Bestow your peace on all, God, hear my plea.

5. O saints of God, hope always in the Lord.
   His steadfast love is ever shed abroad.
   The cross displays his love for all to see.
   Give of its firstfruits, God, hear my plea.

Proper 14/Pentecost 12/Ordinary Time 19
Based on Psalm 130
May be sung to EVENTIDE, 10 10.10 10
LBW 272 — "Abide With Me"

To You, O God, I Come

1. To you, O God, I come in great thanksgiving.
   I praise you for your gracious deeds of love.
   You spread abroad your grace to all the living;
   Great are the works you do, O God, above.

   Refrain
   My thanks and praise I ever give you, God.
   Your works are good. Your works are good.
   My thanks and praise I ever give you, God.
   Your works are good. Your works are good.

2. God of renown, revered in sacred story,
   Your deeds confirm your covenant of grace.
   Honour and majesty convey the glory,
   Yet to be seen when we behold your face. *Refrain*

3. Your greatness, Lord, displayed in acts of wonder,
   Reveal a power; yet, faithful and just.
   Your precepts serve as laws for us to ponder;
   Your uprightness, a way that we can trust. *Refrain*

4. Redemption is your gift to cherish, ever.
   Holy and awesome is your sacred name.
   O Saviour, by your Cross we live forever,
   Always, to praise and render rich acclaim. *Refrain*

Proper 15/Pentecost 13/Ordinary Time 20
Based on Psalm 111
May be sung to O STORE GUD, 11 10.11 10 with refrain (Swedish folk tune)
LBW 532 — "How Great Thou Art"

How Pleasant To Be In God's Presence

1. How pleasant to be in God's presence at prayer!
How lovely to worship, freed from every care!
My soul longs, indeed, for the courts of the Lord.
Joy springs from my heart in the house of our God.

2. The sparrow and swallow find space for their young
At God's altar, nesting, where life was begun.
Oh, happy the creatures in God's vast domain,
Who know their Creator and with him remain.

3. Oh, happy are all in the Lord, finding strength;
Refreshed at God's springs, they shall never grow faint.
Behold God's anointed, against our dread foe,
Our blessed Redeemer, with us as we go.

4. Stir up your full might, Lord, oh, come now to save.
Bring light to our darkness; make hearts to be brave.
Your light on our pathway shall keep our faith strong
To follow you always, while others may scorn.

5. O Lord, hear our prayer and our song of delight.
You favour and honour us, great God of might.
Oh, happy the people who trust in the Lord;
Our sun and shield with us, God ever adored.

Proper 16/Pentecost 14/Ordinary Time 21
Based on Psalm 84
May be sung to ST. DENIO, 11 11.11 11
LBW 526 — "Immortal, Invisible, God Only Wise"

Your Throne, O God, A Place Of Grace

1. Your throne, O God, a place of grace,
From whence all good things flow,
Draws multitudes to seek your face,
And worship in its glow.
That throne, a blessed mercy seat,
Symbolic of your reign,
Compels all evil to retreat,
And Christ, dominion gain.

2. Forever shall your throne endure,
And all your ways be just;
Your royal sceptre, ever sure,
Makes righteousness a must.
Love is the mantel over all,
By which life is best known,
As souls, responsive to your call,
Live in your way, alone.

3. My heart o'erflows, in praise I owe,
My gracious God and King;
As on me, blessings you bestow,
Of you, in joy, I sing.
The oil of gladness marks the one
Who leads us in life's way:
Christ Jesus, whom the vict'ry won,
Remains our hope and stay.

Proper 17/Pentecost 15/Ordinary Time 22
Based on Psalm 45:1-2, 6-9
May be sung to ELLACOMBE, CMD
SBH 308 — "Lift Up Your Heads, Ye Gates Of Brass"

The Mountain Of Our God Shall Stand

1. The mountain of our God shall stand,
Unmoved, remain forever.
God's care shall spread o'er all the land,
And hold us all together.
Mount Zion is the name,
From age to age the same.
Our trust is in its Lord,
Who keeps us by his word,
And claims us as his people.

2. The sceptre of ungodly ways,
Would rule to overpow'r us;
But, to our God belongs all praise:
Thwarts those who would devour us.
God's promise will prevail;
His righteousness not fail.
The gifts God has in store,
Ours shall be evermore,
And we shall be his people.

3. God help us in our earthly strife —
Who render faithful service;
Who keep the covenant through life —
Let nothing ill unnerve us.
Lead evil ones away.
They cannot win the day.
Remove them from our sight.
Lead on, O God of might.
Inspire all your people.

4. Security, God's people know.
   We trust God's word to cheer us,
   As we, unto God's temple go,
   God always will be near us.
   Abounding, full of grace,
   We, there, behold his face.
   Although the way be long,
   His Spirit keeps us strong.
   God gives peace to his people.

Proper 18/Pentecost 16/Ordinary Time 23
Based on Psalm 125
May be sung to EIN FESTE BURG, 87.87.66.667
LBW 229 — "A Mighty Fortress Is Our God"

God's Wonders In Creation

1. God's wonders in creation, revealed from day to day,
Fill lives with fond elation, cause grateful hearts to pray.
There's glory in the heavens, an awesome, star-filled dome,
Where spinning, whirling planets, and galaxies e'er roam.

Refrain
God's glory in creation,
Fills each heart with elation,
Exuding exaltation:
Heaven and earth, our home.

2. The sun that lights each pathway, a steady course does make,
From rising until setting, brightens the way we take.
O light of God, shine onward, lead us to all that's true.
O God of all creation, how good to be with you. *Refrain*

3. God's law conveys a story of precepts ever true,
Enduring is their glory, creating life anew.
Perfection is the watchword, that shines in each decree,
Reviving soul and spirit, unto eternity. *Refrain*

Proper 19/Pentecost 17/Ordinary Time 24
Based on Psalm 19
May be sung to HANKEY, 76.76 D with *refrain*
LBW 390 — "I Love To Tell The Story"

Happy, The Life God Gives

Refrain
Happy, the life God gives to us,
Wherein, we know sweet peace;
Happy, the life God gives to us,
Where joys shall never cease.

1. Two ways there are to travel:
One right, the other wrong.
Travel the way with Jesus,
He'll guide you all life long. *Refrain*

2. There's a way that makes me happy,
It's the way of God's delight;
And all those who travel with him,
Will prosper, doing right. *Refrain*

3. The wicked soon are scattered,
Like chaff, are blown away.
The righteous are well planted,
And bear fruit in their day. *Refrain*

Proper 20/Pentecost 18/Ordinary Time 25
Based on Psalm 1
May be sung to BALM IN GILEAD (irregular)
WOV 737 — "There Is A Balm In Gilead"

Help Is Ours In The Lord

1. Help is ours in the Lord,
    in his name, rich reward:
  Saving life, giving hope, on our side.
  There is naught we should fear,
    with the Lord ever near.
  Help is ours, in the name of the Lord.

2. Oh, to God, be all praise,
    acting from ancient days,
  Giving strength to the weak and distressed.
  The oppressed were set free
    as they passed through the sea.
  Help is ours, in the name of the Lord.

3. With the Lord on our side,
    our creator and guide,
  We are helped every step of life's way.
  Through the storms, through all strife,
    God protects us through life.
  Help is ours, in the name of the Lord.

Proper 21/Pentecost 19/Ordinary Time 26
Based on Psalm 124
May be sung to PRECIOUS LORD, 12 9.12 9 (irregular)
WOV 731 — "Precious Lord, Take My Hand"

God, My Judge, I Stand Before You

1. God, my judge, I stand before you,
Trusting in your steadfast ways;
Knowing you will vindicate me,
For your justice, I give praise.
As I walk, in faith, beside you,
May my heart know blessed peace.
May my heart know blessed peace.

2. Lord, I come into your presence,
Giving thanks in joyful song.
At your altar, grace surrounds me;
By your Spirit I'm made strong.
All your deeds proclaim your glory,
Wondrous are the things you do.
Wondrous are the things you do.

3. How I love your house of worship
Where your glory, Lord, abides.
In the company of others,
Truly, faithfulness resides.
As we join in celebration,
Great redeemer, bless us all.
Great redeemer, bless us all.

Proper 22/Pentecost 20/Ordinary Time 27
Based on Psalm 26
May be sung to CWM RHONDDA, 87.87.877
LBW 343 — "Guide Me, Ever, Great Redeemer"

God Has Done Great Things

Refrain
God has done great things for us,
In which we all rejoice.
For the blessings heaped on us,
We praise God, as one voice.

1. God is the cause of laughter,
And source of all our joy.
We praise God with thanksgiving:
Naught can our faith destroy. *Refrain*

2. Weeping gives way to praising;
Tears are displaced by peace,
As God restores our fortunes,
And grants our souls' release. *Refrain*

3. God's deeds of restoration,
Were known in ages past:
The Lord delivered Zion,
And dreams came true at last. *Refrain*

4. Our faith is in the future,
As by the Lord we're led;
A people blessed and nourished,
And by God's hand, well fed. *Refrain*

Thanksgiving Day
(Canada in October; USA in November)
Based on Psalm 126
May be sung to ROYAL OAK, 76.76 with *refrain*
WOV 767 — "All Things Bright And Beautiful"

O God, I Cry To You

1. O God, I cry to you, beset with anguish.
Groaning I make my plea, in great distress.
While I am waiting here, distraught I languish.
Will you not answer? I crave your caress.

2. Have you forsaken me? Left me to wander?
Do you not hear my call? Answer is none.
Out of the depths I wail; hope cast asunder.
Hear me, I pray you. When will your help come?

3. Yet, Lord, in you I trust, knowing your story,
As I remember your grace in the past:
To you our people cried. You showed your glory.
In great deliv'rence, they found peace at last.

4. I trust you, Lord, to be faithful forever.
As in the past, so now, my helper be.
O Lord, be near by side, forsake me never.
In pow'r and mercy, O Lord, set me free.

Proper 23/Pentecost 21/Ordinary Time 28
Based on Psalm 22:1-15
May be sung to CONSOLATOR, 11 10.11 10
SBH 569 — "Come, Ye Disconsolate"

Creator God, We Praise Your Name

1. Creator God, we praise your name.
How awesome are the works you do!
Eternal is your vast domain.
Each soul responds in thanks to you.

2. The heavens, massive pow'r display,
From glowing sun to distant star;
Created splendour, night and day,
Leading our utmost thoughts afar.

3. The earth, our home, rolls on through space,
Centre of your creative plan,
Set to sustain the human race.
For this, we praise as best we can.

4. How manifold, the works we view.
In wisdom you have made them all.
The creatures owe their lives to you
Sharing of your great banquet hall.

5. Praise, with thanksgiving, Lord, we give,
For what is now and yet shall be.
We bless you, Lord, and with you live,
Secure, unto eternity.

Proper 24/Pentecost 22/Ordinary Time 29
Based on Psalm 104:1-9, 24, 35c
May be sung to OLD HUNDREDTH, LM
SBH 161 — "Before Jehovah's Awful Throne"

Give Blessing To God

1. Give blessing to God, the star of creation.
   Give blessing to God, the star of creation.
   Give blessing to God, the star of creation.
   Give blessing to God. Give blessing to God.

2. Oh, magnify God, the Lord of each nation.
   Oh, magnify God, the Lord of each nation.
   Oh, magnify God, the Lord of each nation.
   Oh, magnify God. Oh, magnify God.

3. Oh, taste, God is good. Oh, savour God's goodness.
   Oh, taste, God is good. Oh, savour God's goodness.
   Oh, taste, God is good. Oh, savour God's goodness.
   Oh, taste, God is good. Oh, taste, God is good.

4. Oh, look to the Lord. Oh, see the redeemer.
   Oh, look to the Lord. Oh, see the redeemer.
   Oh, look to the Lord. Oh, see the redeemer.
   Oh, look to the Lord. Oh, look to the Lord.

5. Give praise to our Lord, rejoice with thanksgiving.
   Give praise to our Lord, rejoice with thanksgiving.
   Give praise to our Lord, rejoice with thanksgiving.
   Give praise to our Lord. Give praise to our Lord.

Proper 25/Pentecost 23/Ordinary Time 30
Based on Psalm 34:1-8 (19-22)
May be sung to CANTARD AL SENÕR, 56 56.56 55
WOV 795 — "Oh, Sing To The Lord" (Brazilian folk tune)

How Good It Is To Live As One

1. How good it is to live as one
In unity and love,
With Christ, the Word, renewing us,
Fit for God's courts above.

2. How very good and pleasant, too,
Community can be,
When, in the peace of Christ we know,
Mercy that sets us free.

3. Like precious oil poured on the head,
Bestowed on honoured guest,
So is the honour God bestows,
Wherein we find sweet rest.

4. The dew of Herman falls so fine
On Zion's lofty mount,
And, in its cool refreshing balm,
We're blessed by God's own fount.

5. From Zion's height, God lifts us up,
His blessing there to give:
Eternal life God offers all,
As by his grace we live.

6. We all are one, and Christ in all,
United in him, stand —
Christ's kindred in the life we share,
Held firm by God's strong hand.

Reformation Day
Based on Psalm 133
May be sung to DUNLOPS CREEK, CM
WOV 675 — "We Walk By Faith And Not By Sight"

Creation's God Reigning In Splendour

1. Creation's God, reigning in splendour,
   Oh, what a glorious sight to behold.
   Lord of the world and all that's in it,
   All of earth's people, the good shepherd's fold.

   Refrain
   The King of Glory, the Lord of all life.
   Our God forever. Alleluia!

2. God's holy hill, where the saints gather,
   All the redeemed cleansed by Jesus, God's Son.
   In white array, praising the Holy
   God, the almighty, the great three-in-one. *Refrain*

3. Seeing God's face, oh, what a blessing;
   Naught can compare to the glory revealed.
   Now is fulfilled every soul's longing.
   In the Lord's presence there's nothing concealed. *Refrain*

4. Doors stand ajar; gates flung wide open,
   Lifted on high that the Lord may go in.
   Followed by saints from every nation,
   All of one spirit and each other's kin. *Refrain*

5. Visions behold; truths never ending;
   Christ reigns in triumph, in heaven above.
   All is fulfilled, God's word enduring.
   Saints know the joy of most wonderful love. *Refrain*

All Saints
Based on Psalm 24
May be sung to EARTH AND ALL STARS, 457.457 with *refrain*
WOV 674 — "Alleluia! Jesus Is Risen"

Praise To The Lord

1. Praise to the Lord, my soul delights in praising
The one who keeps me ever in his care.
So shall my voice of praise ever be raising
Glad songs, in thanks, for showing how to share.
O Lord, my God, above all earthly powers,
You rule in love and bless with every grace.
Praise to the Lord, whose love fills all my hours;
My praise I give 'til I behold your face.

2. Praise to the Lord, who made the earth and heaven;
In justice rules, from heaven's mercy seat.
God's love is known in all things, like a leaven.
God holds us up, his strong arms underneath.
Happy are they who live within God's keeping;
Who know the joy of care both day and night.
Praise to the Lord! We live, his will e'er seeking,
And raise our songs to God with all our might.

3. Praise to the Lord, whose love abounds forever:
The hungry feeds, and sets the prisoner free;
Helps orphans, too; the widow's care, his pleasure;
And what delight! He makes the blind to see.
O God, you reign throughout all generations,
Loving the right, and lifting those bowed down.
Praise to the Lord, the song of all the nations.
Praise to the Lord, bless God who wears the crown.

Proper 26/Pentecost 24/Ordinary Time 31
Based on Psalm 146
May be sung to LONDONDERRY AIR, 11 10.11 10 D
WOV 778 — "O Christ The Same"

How Peaceful The Family With Whom The Lord Dwells

1. How peaceful the family with whom the Lord dwells.
   Security marks his control.
   Responding in faith to the good news he tells
   Is assurance God guards well my soul.

2. In building a house, or whatever you do —
   No matter the effort applied —
   Unless God is part of the plan you pursue,
   All is vanity, laced with false pride.

3. The heritage given by God in a home:
   The fruit of the womb, a reward.
   No joy can compare, underneath heaven's dome,
   With such gifts from the hand of the Lord.

4. The house of the Lord where the Spirit abides —
   A happy abode for us all —
   Assurance conveys to each one who confides
   In the Lord, by whose strength we stand tall.

Proper 27/Pentecost 25/Ordinary Time 32
Based on Psalm 127
May be sung to IT IS WELL, 11 8.11 9
LBW 346 — "When Peace, Like A River"

Oh, To God Alone Be Glory

1. Oh, to God alone be glory, for his tender, loving care.
   Earth unfolds a sacred story: God is active everywhere.
   Oh, my heart exudes thanksgiving, and my mouth gives way to praise,
   To my God, who, ever-living, grants me vict'ry all my days.

2. Holy One, God like no other; none beside you can compare.
   Friend that's closer than a brother: Rock of ages, always there.
   You, our God the Lord, all-knowing, work to set all things aright.
   In the balance — justice showing, as you rule, our God of might.

3. Earthly fortunes lose their power; tables oft are overturned;
   Changes come and go each hour, as reversals are discerned.
   All the ways of life, unfolding, show our God is in control.
   In his strong arms, ever holding, each one, dear, a precious soul.

4. From on high the Lord will thunder, as the mighty are put down.
   Evil will be rent asunder; God's anointed, wear the crown.
   All God's ways of love shall flourish as the faithful find their place,
   Seated where the Lord will nourish all the loved ones, by his grace.

Proper 28/Pentecost 26/Ordinary Time 33
Based on 1 Samuel 2:1-10
May be sung to AUSTRIA, 87.87 D
LBW 358 — "Glories Of Your Name Are Spoken"

The Reign Of Christ Is Here

1. The reign of Christ is here!
Good Christian friends, draw near.
The Son of God, acclaim —
The mighty servant — Lord,
The king ever adored.
The Son of God, acclaim.

2. Of Jesus Christ we sing,
And with our praises bring
Rich blessings to his name.
Bow down before his throne.
Oh, worship him, alone.
The Son of God, acclaim.

3. Let all God's faithful cry,
Praise to the Lord on high.
Jesus shall ever reign.
Raised up, a horn to be,
Blest through eternity.
The Son of God acclaim.

4. God's own anointed Son,
Highly exalted one,
Removes all sin and shame.
Salvation through the tree,
Our gain shall ever be.
The Son of God, acclaim.

5. The lamp of God, so bright,
Shines out eternal light,
That first to this world came.
To him who wears the crown,
Streams forth words of renown.
The Son of God, acclaim.

6. O servants, one and all,
   Responding to God's call,
   Give honour to Christ's name.
   May Zion's walls resound,
   With praises that abound.
   The Son of God, acclaim.

Christ The King/Proper 29
Based on Psalm 132:1-12 (13-18)
May be sung to LAUDES DOMINI, 666.666
LBW 546 — "When Morning Gilds The Skies"

www.ingramcontent.com/pod-product-compliance
Lightning Source LLC
LaVergne TN
LVHW020653100826
845148LV00012B/2470

* 9 7 8 0 7 8 8 0 2 5 5 0 1 *